pasta

COMFORT FOOD

pasta
COMFORT FOOD

MELISSA CLARK

Andrews McMeel
Publishing

Kansas City

ISBN: 0-8362-5115-6

Library of Congress Catalog Card Number: 97-73615

First Edition

1 2 3 4 5 6 7 8 9 10

Produced by Smallwood & Stewart, Inc., New York City

Editor: Deborah Mintcheff

Copy Editor: Judith Sutton

Designer: Susi Oberhelman

Design Assistant: Ayako Hosono

Photographer: Steven Mark Needham

Food Stylist: William Smith

Jacket photograph: Savory Beef & Sausage Ragu

Back jacket photograph: Salmon with Tagliatelle & Fried Leeks

Page 2 photograph: Baked Ziti with Veal & Mozzarella

table of contents

When it came to food, my parents were always ahead of their time. Disciples of Julia Child, they followed every emerging food trend and novelty with an almost religious devotion. Not surprisingly, therefore, they were the first in our neighborhood to own a pasta machine. Endless hours were spent happily rolling out golden strands of egg fettuccine, which they hung to dry, streaming like Rapunzel's locks down the backs of our kitchen chairs.

Growing up in such a household indelibly marked me. I never thought of food simply as a way to nourish the body, but rather as nourishment for one's senses and soul. Food was our common language, and now as a writer, it is the language I use to express myself, though I'm not sure that my love of pasta would have developed if not for my husband's influence.

Paul is from an Italian family and his grandmother always made hundreds of cheese-filled ravioli for every family occasion. Grandma Pasqualena mixed the dough by hand, kneading together a mound of imported flour and fresh eggs on the kitchen table. After rolling and filling, she would lay the finished ravioli to dry on a bedsheet set aside specifically for that purpose.

Following in his grandmother's flour-dusted footsteps, Paul impressed me by unearthing my own pasta machine (which was still in its box), and rolling out velvety, soft sheets of pasta, which he cut into squares and deftly rolled around a chopstick to form penne quills. The sauce, he suggested, would be my contribution to the meal.

It is an arrangement we still adhere to, and my repertoire of sauces grows and changes with the passing of the seasons and with each fresh batch of pasta. Some of the dishes presented here are Italian family favorites and others are innovations. They work equally well with fresh or good-quality dried pasta.

Pasta has become a universally popular comfort food. Not only is it satisfying, but it is also versatile—ideal for any meal, whatever the season. Its myriad shapes allow us to indulge our mood for one type over another and matching pastas and sauces appropriately makes the eating experience more pleasurable. The chart on page 78 suggests classic combinations—light sauces are paired with delicate shapes, hearty sauces are supported by sturdier pasta.

When choosing a recipe, consider the season. Pastas with delicate herbs and asparagus are best in spring; cool pasta salads are ideal in summer; use recipes calling for eggplant, tomatoes, and peppers in the late summer and fall when farmers' markets are overflowing with produce; hearty cheese and meat-flavored pastas are fall and winter favorites, warming against the winds and icy chill.

Here, I offer a deeply personal collection of sauces and pasta dishes that I happily and eagerly share with you. I hope you enjoy them as much as we do.

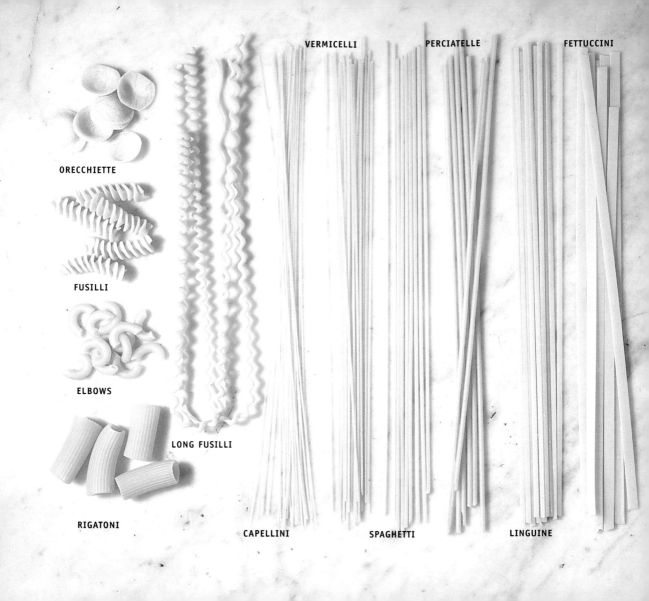

ORECCHIETTE

FUSILLI

ELBOWS

RIGATONI

LONG FUSILLI

VERMICELLI

CAPELLINI

PERCIATELLE

SPAGHETTI

FETTUCCINI

LINGUINE

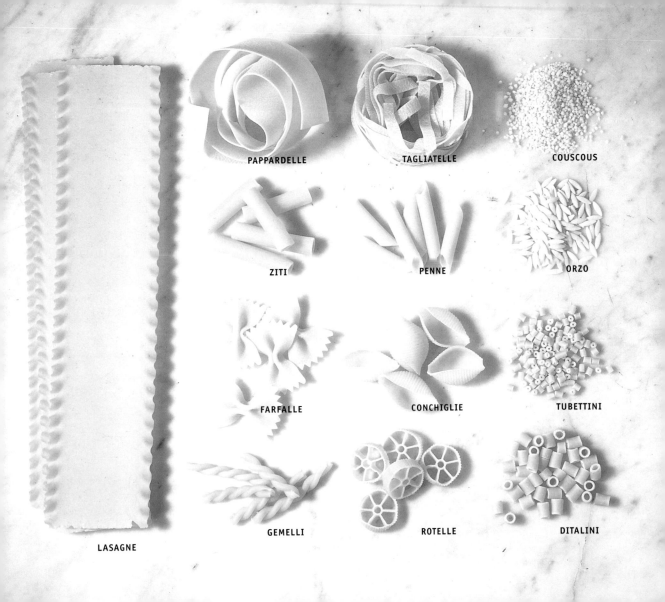

PAPPARDELLE

TAGLIATELLE

COUSCOUS

ZITI

PENNE

ORZO

FARFALLE

CONCHIGLIE

TUBETTINI

GEMELLI

ROTELLE

DITALINI

LASAGNE

pasta with deconstructed pesto

This verdant dish has all the vibrant flavors of pesto sauce without the usual pounding. Toasting the pine nuts imparts a rich, nutty nuance that rounds out the flavors.

Cook the pasta following the basic method (p. 52).

Meanwhile, prepare the pesto: In a small skillet, heat 2 tablespoons of the oil over medium-high heat. Add the pine nuts and saute for 2 to 3 minutes, until golden brown. Set the pine nuts aside.

Drain the pasta, then transfer to a large serving bowl. Add the basil, Parmesan, pine nuts, garlic, and the remaining ⅓ cup oil. Season with salt and pepper and toss until mixed.

SERVES 4 TO 6

1 pound pasta, any type

PESTO

⅓ cup plus 2 tablespoons extra-virgin olive oil

¼ cup pine nuts

2 cups lightly packed torn fresh basil leaves

⅓ cup freshly grated Parmesan cheese

4 large garlic cloves, minced

Salt & freshly ground pepper

spaghetti aglio e olio

1 pound spaghetti
  or linguine

AGLIO E OLIO

½ cup extra-virgin
  olive oil

7 large garlic cloves,
  thinly sliced

Pinch of crushed red
  pepper flakes

1 tablespoon fresh
  lemon juice

Salt & freshly ground
  pepper

2 tablespoons chopped
  fresh flat-leaf parsley,
  for garnish

Though this is one of the most elemental ways to serve pasta, the combination of lightly browned garlic and fruity olive oil makes it nonetheless one of the most comforting.

Cook the pasta following the basic method (p. 52).

Meanwhile, prepare the aglio e olio: In a large deep skillet, heat the oil over medium-high heat. Add the garlic and red pepper flakes and saute for 2 minutes, or until the garlic is translucent. Remove from the heat, add the lemon juice, and season with salt and pepper. (The garlic will continue to cook and turn golden brown in the hot oil.)

Drain the pasta and transfer to the skillet. Toss over medium heat for about 1 minute, or until well coated. Transfer to a large serving bowl, sprinkle with the parsley, and serve.

SERVES 4 TO 6

spaghetti alla carbonara

This dish finds its humble origins in the mountains of Italy, where it is said that the charcoal makers (carbonare) *prepared it as a speedy but satisfying dinner.*

In a large skillet, melt the butter with the oil over medium-high heat. Add the pancetta and onion and saute for 4 minutes, or until the pancetta is cooked but not browned. Pour in the wine and deglaze the pan by bringing the mixture to a boil and scraping to loosen any browned bits in the bottom of the pan. Cook until most of the liquid has evaporated.

Cook the pasta following the basic method (p. 52).

Meanwhile, in a large serving bowl, whisk together the Parmesan, Romano, egg yolks, and parsley, and season with salt and pepper. Set the bowl near the stove.

Drain the pasta, reserving ¼ cup of the pasta water. Transfer the hot pasta and the pancetta mixture to the serving bowl, tossing and adding the reserved pasta water, 1 tablespoon at a time if needed. Serve immediately. **SERVES 4 TO 6**

- **2 tablespoons butter**
- **2 tablespoons extra-virgin olive oil**
- **¼ pound thinly sliced pancetta, cut crosswise into thin strips**
- **¼ cup chopped onion**
- **⅓ cup dry white wine**
- **1 pound spaghetti or linguine**
- **½ cup freshly grated Parmesan cheese**
- **¼ cup freshly grated Pecorino Romano cheese**
- **4 large egg yolks**
- **2 tablespoons chopped fresh flat-leaf parsley**
- **Salt & freshly ground pepper**

spaghetti alla puttanesca bianca

1 pound pasta, such as spaghetti or linguine

PUTTANESCA BIANCA

¼ cup extra-virgin olive oil

½ cup brine-cured black olives, pitted & finely chopped

4 anchovy fillets, finely chopped

2 tablespoons capers, finely chopped

4 large garlic cloves, minced

⅛ teaspoon crushed red pepper flakes

Salt & freshly ground pepper

⅓ cup pale green celery leaves, coarsely chopped, for garnish

In this variation on the classic sauce, puttanesca is prepared without tomato, which allows the enticing, pungent flavors of the capers, olives, garlic, and anchovies to shine through.

Cook the pasta following the basic method (p. 52). Drain well, reserving ¼ cup of the pasta water.

Meanwhile, prepare the puttanesca bianca: In a large skillet, heat the oil over medium-high heat. Add the olives, anchovies, capers, and garlic and saute for 2 to 3 minutes, until the garlic is golden brown. Stir in the red pepper flakes and season with salt and pepper.

Add the pasta to the sauce and toss until mixed. If the pasta seems dry, stir in some of the reserved pasta water, 1 tablespoon at a time. Transfer to a large serving bowl and sprinkle with the celery leaves. **SERVES 4 TO 6**

fettuccine al limone

1 pound fettuccine or tagliatelle

¼ cup (½ stick) butter

½ cup heavy cream

Zest of 3 lemons, removed in strips with a vegetable peeler & cut crosswise into fine shreds

2 tablespoons fresh lemon juice

¾ cup freshly grated Parmesan cheese

Salt & freshly ground pepper

Pinch of freshly grated nutmeg

The sublime combination of fresh lemon juice, Parmesan cheese, and cream may seem more like an innovation than traditional Italian fare, but it is actually a classic combination that deserves to be rediscovered and embraced by pasta enthusiasts.

Cook the pasta following the basic method (p. 52).

Meanwhile, in a large skillet, melt the butter over medium-high heat. Add the cream and bring to a boil. Stir in the lemon zest and juice. Simmer for about 4 minutes, or until the cream is reduced by half.

Drain the pasta, reserving ¼ cup of the pasta water. Transfer the pasta to the skillet. Add the Parmesan, season with salt and pepper, and toss until the pasta is mixed well, adding some of the reserved pasta water, 1 tablespoon at a time, if the mixture seems dry. Transfer the pasta to a large serving bowl and sprinkle evenly with the nutmeg. **SERVES 4 TO 6**

pasta with quick tomato-basil sauce

Not all tomato sauces are long-simmered. This lively, fresh-tasting sauce cooks in just 15 minutes.

Prepare the tomato-basil sauce: In a large deep skillet, heat the oil over medium-high heat. Add the garlic and saute for 1 minute, or until fragrant. Add the tomatoes and their juice and bring to a simmer. Cook the sauce, uncovered, stirring occasionally, for about 15 minutes, or until slightly thickened. Stir in the basil and season with salt and pepper.

Meanwhile, cook the pasta following the basic method (p. 52). Drain well. Add the pasta to the skillet, toss until well coated with the sauce, and transfer to a large serving bowl. Pass the Parmesan on the side. **SERVES 4 TO 6**

TOMATO-BASIL SAUCE

2 tablespoons extra-virgin olive oil

2 large garlic cloves, minced

1 (28-ounce) can whole tomatoes, drained & chopped, juice reserved

¼ cup chopped fresh basil

Salt & freshly ground pepper

1 pound pasta, any type

Freshly grated Parmesan cheese, for serving

pasta with slow-cooked marinara

MARINARA SAUCE

3 tablespoons olive oil

1 small onion, sliced

1 carrot, chopped

1 celery stalk, chopped

3 large garlic cloves, minced

1 (28-ounce) can crushed tomatoes

1 tablespoon tomato paste

1 bay leaf

3 tablespoons chopped fresh flat-leaf parsley

Salt & freshly ground pepper

1 pound pasta, any type

Freshly grated Parmesan cheese, for serving

The longer cooking time of this sauce results in full-bodied flavor that is only possible when vegetables are allowed to caramelize slowly.

Prepare the marinara sauce: In a large skillet, heat the oil over medium-high heat. Add the onion, reduce the heat to medium-low, and cook, stirring, for 20 minutes, or until the onion is deep golden brown. Add the carrot and celery and cook for 5 minutes, or until the celery is softened. Add the garlic and saute for 1 minute longer, or until fragrant.

Stir in the tomatoes, tomato paste, and bay leaf and bring to a simmer. Cook the sauce, stirring occasionally, for 30 minutes, or until thickened. Remove the bay leaf, stir in the parsley, and season with salt and pepper.

Meanwhile, cook the pasta following the basic method (p. 52). Drain well and return the pasta to the pot. Add the sauce and over medium heat, toss until the pasta is well coated. Transfer to a large serving bowl and pass the Parmesan separately. **SERVES 4 TO 6**

penne all'arrabbiata

Given the generous dose of fiery crushed red pepper flakes and garlic in this classic tomato-based sauce, it's not surprising that arrabbiata *means "angry" in Italian.*

Prepare the arrabbiata sauce: In a large skillet, heat the oil over medium-high heat. Add the garlic and red pepper flakes and saute for 2 minutes, or until fragrant. Add the tomatoes and bring to a simmer. Cook the sauce, uncovered, stirring occasionally, for 20 minutes, or until slightly thickened. Stir in the parsley and season with salt and pepper.

Meanwhile, cook the pasta following the basic method (p. 52). Drain well. Transfer the pasta to the skillet and toss with the sauce over medium heat until well coated. Spoon into a large serving bowl. **SERVES 4 TO 6**

ARRABBIATA SAUCE

- ¼ cup extra-virgin olive oil
- 5 large garlic cloves, thinly sliced
- ½ teaspoon crushed red pepper flakes
- 1 (28-ounce) can crushed tomatoes
- ⅓ cup chopped fresh flat-leaf parsley
- Salt & freshly ground pepper

- 1 pound penne or penne rigate

squash & spinach soup with ditalini

3 tablespoons butter

1 medium-size onion, chopped

3 medium-size yellow squash, cut into ¾-inch chunks

1 pound all-purpose potatoes, peeled & cut into ¾-inch chunks

1 pound spinach, trimmed, washed well & coarsely chopped

2 cups chicken broth

2 cups cold water

1 cup ditalini or tubetti

¾ teaspoon salt

Freshly ground pepper

This delicately flavored, pale green soup is thickened with potato instead of the more usual cream, giving it a velvety texture without the added calories.

In a large saucepan, melt the butter over medium heat. Add the onion and squash and saute for 3 to 4 minutes, until softened. Add the potatoes and spinach, stirring well to coat with the butter. Add the broth and water and bring to a boil. Reduce the heat to low and simmer for 20 minutes, or until the vegetables are very tender.

Meanwhile, cook the pasta following the basic method (p. 52). Drain well, then briefly rinse under cold water.

Using a slotted spoon, transfer the vegetables to a food processor or blender and puree. Return the vegetable puree to the saucepan and stir until the soup is well blended. Add the pasta, salt, and pepper. Gently reheat the soup over low heat before serving. **SERVES 6 TO 8**

pasta e fagiole

2 cups dried
  cannellini beans

2 bay leaves

¼ cup olive oil

1 onion, chopped

2 celery stalks,
  chopped

1 carrot, chopped

¼ pound sliced pro-
  sciutto, cut in strips

5 large garlic cloves,
  minced

1 (28-ounce) can
  tomatoes

¼ cup chopped fresh
  flat-leaf parsley

½ teaspoon dried
  oregano

2 cups beef broth

Salt & pepper

½ pound ditalini

Freshly grated
  Parmesan cheese

There are probably as many versions of this classic soup as there are Italian cooks. Here's my favorite rendition, which combines white cannellini beans with prosciutto and tomatoes.

In a large bowl, soak the beans overnight in water to cover by 3 inches. Drain well and rinse thoroughly.

In a large pot, combine the beans, 8 cups cold water, and the bay leaves. Bring to a boil. Reduce the heat and simmer, partially covered, for 1 hour, or until the beans are tender.

In a large skillet, heat the oil over medium heat. Add the onion, celery, and carrot and cook for 5 minutes, or until the onion is softened. Add the prosciutto and garlic; cook for 2 minutes longer. Break up the tomatoes and add with their juice. Simmer, stirring, for 20 minutes. Stir in the parsley and oregano.

Add the tomato mixture and broth to the beans. Simmer for 30 minutes. Season with salt and pepper, add the pasta, and cook for 10 minutes, until the pasta is al dente. Ladle into large bowls and pass the Parmesan on the side. **SERVES 8**

spicy chicken broth with peas & ham

Pure comfort food, this warming, country-style soup is brimming with tender vegetables in a lemony pepper-spiced broth.

In a large saucepan, heat the oil over medium heat. Add the ham, onion, celery, and carrot and saute for 5 minutes, or until the onion is softened. Add the garlic and saute for 1 minute longer, or until the garlic is translucent. Add the red pepper flakes and season with salt and pepper. Stir in the broth and bring to a boil. Reduce the heat to low and simmer for about 10 minutes.

Raise the heat to medium and stir in the tubetti and peas. Cook for about 10 minutes longer, or until the vegetables are tender and the tubetti is al dente. Stir in the chives and the lemon zest.

Ladle the soup into deep bowls and serve the Romano on the side. SERVES 6 TO 8

3 tablespoons olive oil

¼ pound smoked ham, cut into ½-inch cubes

1 medium-size onion, chopped

1 celery stalk & 1 carrot, cut into ¼-inch dice

5 large garlic cloves, thinly sliced

¾ teaspoon crushed red pepper flakes

Salt & freshly ground pepper

6 cups chicken broth

2 cups tubetti

1 cup frozen peas, thawed

2 tablespoons snipped fresh chives

1 teaspoon grated lemon zest

Freshly grated Romano cheese, for serving

moroccan vermicelli & chickpea soup

- 2 tablespoons butter, plus additional if needed
- 2 tablespoons olive oil, plus additional if needed
- 8 chicken thighs (about 2 pounds), skin removed
- ½ pound boneless lamb shoulder, cut into 1-inch chunks
- Salt & freshly ground pepper
- 1 large onion, chopped
- 4 celery stalks with leaves, finely chopped
- 3 large garlic cloves, minced
- 1 teaspoon turmeric
- ½ teaspoon ground coriander
- ½ teaspoon crushed red pepper flakes

This thick, peppery soup is based on the Moroccan specialty harira, *a dish that is enjoyed all year around. It is especially popular during Ramadan, when it is eaten to break the daily fast that lasts until sundown during the month-long religious holiday.*

In a large pot, melt the butter with the oil over medium-high heat. Season the chicken and lamb with salt and pepper. Working in batches, brown the chicken well on all sides, transferring it to a platter as it browns. Brown the lamb, using additional butter and oil if needed, and transferring it to the platter with the chicken.

Add the onion and celery to the pot and saute for about 5 minutes, or until the onion is softened. Add the garlic, turmeric, coriander, and red pepper flakes, and season with salt and ½ teaspoon pepper. Saute for 1 minute longer, or until the garlic is translucent. Return the chicken and lamb, along with any accumulated juices, to the pot. Add the tomatoes, broth, water, and cinnamon stick. Bring to a boil, then reduce the heat to low and let simmer, partially covered, for 50 minutes.

Add the chickpeas and simmer for 15 minutes longer, or until the lamb is fork-tender.

Using a slotted spoon, transfer the chicken thighs to a plate. When cool enough to handle, remove the chicken meat from the bones and cut into bite-sized pieces. Discard the bones and return the chicken to the pot.

Bring the soup to a simmer. Add the vermicelli and cook for 10 minutes, or until the vermicelli is al dente. Stir in the parsley, cilantro, and lemon juice. Ladle the soup into large shallow bowls and garnish with lemon wedges. **SERVES 6**

1 (28-ounce) can crushed tomatoes

3 cups chicken broth

3 cups cold water

One 2-inch piece cinnamon stick

1 (15-ounce) can chickpeas, drained & rinsed

2 ounces egg vermicelli, broken into 2-inch lengths

¼ cup chopped fresh flat-leaf parsley

¼ cup chopped fresh cilantro

2 tablespoons fresh lemon juice

Lemon wedges, for garnish

roasted-cherry
tomato pasta salad

Roasting tomatoes intensifies their deep,
sweet flavor. For a heartier version, add
some slivers of thinly sliced prosciutto
to the salad along with the tarragon.

Preheat the oven to 450°F.

In a large shallow baking dish, toss the tomatoes with 2 tablespoons of the oil and season with salt and pepper. Spread the tomatoes in a single layer and roast them, stirring once, for about 8 minutes, or until lightly browned. Set aside.

Meanwhile, cook the pasta following the basic method (p. 52). Drain well, then transfer to a large bowl. Add the remaining ¼ cup oil, the garlic, and season with salt and pepper; toss well. Set aside to cool completely.

Add 1 tablespoon vinegar to the pasta and toss. Season to taste with salt, pepper, and additional vinegar if necessary. Add the roasted tomatoes and the tarragon and toss until mixed. Arrange the radicchio leaves on serving plates and spoon the pasta salad on top. **SERVES 6 TO 8**

2 pints cherry tomatoes

¼ cup plus 2 tablespoons extra-virgin olive oil

Salt & freshly ground pepper

1 pound penne or ziti

1 large garlic clove, minced

1 to 2 tablespoons balsamic vinegar

¼ cup chopped fresh tarragon

1 medium-size head radicchio or red leaf lettuce, separated into leaves

muffaletta pasta salad

½ pound farfalle or rotelle

¼ cup olive oil

1½ tablespoons red wine vinegar

2 peperoncini, minced

2 garlic cloves, minced

1 scallion, thinly sliced

2 tablespoons chopped fresh parsley

Salt & freshly ground pepper

1 tomato, seeded & cut into ½-inch dice, juice reserved

½ cup diced green bell pepper

¼ cup coarsely chopped pitted green olives

1 ounce each sliced hard salami & provolone, cut into thin strips

3 cups lightly packed shredded romaine lettuce (about 3 cups)

A muffaletta is one of many New Orleans specialties inspired by the Italian immigrants who settled there in the late nineteenth century. Here, I've eliminated the bread and turned the sandwich's filling into a hearty, full-flavored pasta salad that keeps and carries well.

Cook the pasta following the basic method (p. 52). Drain well.

Meanwhile, in a large bowl, whisk together the oil, vinegar, peperoncini, garlic, scallion, and parsley. Season to taste with salt and pepper.

Add the dressing to the warm pasta, toss well, and set aside for 20 minutes to allow the pasta to cool and absorb some of the dressing.

Add the tomato, bell pepper, olives, salami, and provolone to the pasta and gently mix.

To serve, line individual plates with the lettuce and top with the pasta salad. **SERVES 2 TO 4**

pumpkin tortelloni with cilantro vinaigrette

Make this spunky, Southwestern-inspired salad during the summer when both sweet, fresh corn and ripe, juicy tomatoes are abundant and at their best.

In a large pot, bring 4 quarts of water to a boil over high heat. Add 2 tablespoons salt and the tortelloni. Cook, stirring occasionally, for 6 to 8 minutes, then add the corn and cook for 30 seconds longer. Drain the tortelloni and corn in a colander and set aside.

In a food processor or blender, combine the oil, lime juice, jalapeño, cilantro, and garlic, and season with salt and pepper; process until smooth. Transfer the dressing to a large bowl. Add the tortelloni and corn, the tomato, and scallion, tossing well. Season to taste with salt and pepper if necessary.

To serve, transfer the tortelloni salad to a large serving platter and scatter the avocado over the top. **SERVES 4**

NOTE

Pumpkin tortelloni is available in specialty food stores.

Salt

1 pound **pumpkin tortelloni** (*see Note*)

2 ears **fresh corn,** kernels cut off

¼ cup plus 1 tablespoon **extra-virgin olive oil**

3 tablespoons **fresh lime juice**

1 medium-size **jalapeño chile,** halved & seeded

¼ cup finely chopped **fresh cilantro**

2 large **garlic cloves,** minced

Freshly ground **pepper**

1 small **tomato,** peeled, seeded & cut into ½-inch dice

1 **scallion,** thinly sliced

1 ripe **avocado,** halved, pitted, peeled & cut into ½-inch cubes

six-herb
pasta salad

1 pound conchiglie

⅓ cup extra-virgin olive oil

2 tablespoons fresh lemon juice

Salt & freshly ground pepper

6 ounces fresh goat cheese, crumbled (about 1½ cups)

½ cup mixed chopped fresh herbs, such as chives, parsley, mint, marjoram, chervil, basil, and thyme

This is summertime comfort food at its best. The velvety smooth goat cheese tossed with the fresh herbs makes for simple but satisfying food. If you have a home garden, gathering six different herbs won't be a problem. If you don't, simply use as many fresh herbs as you can find.

Cook the pasta following the basic method (p. 52). Drain well, then transfer to a large serving bowl. Add the oil, lemon juice, ½ teaspoon salt, and ¼ teaspoon pepper, tossing well. Set aside for at least 20 minutes or up to 2 hours.

Add the goat cheese and herbs to the pasta and lightly toss. Season to taste with salt and pepper if needed. Toss the pasta again, divide among large shallow bowls, and serve.

SERVES 4 TO 6

linguine with black pepper bread crumbs

1 pound linguine

¼ cup (½ stick) butter

2 cups fresh bread crumbs

1½ to 2 teaspoons very coarsely ground pepper

1 cup freshly grated Pecorino Romano cheese (4 ounces)

Salt

In this easily prepared dish, buttered bread crumbs soften the bite of black pepper and the salty tang of the sheep's cheese. For the best results, adjust your pepper grinder to its coarsest setting.

Cook the pasta following the basic method (p. 52).

Meanwhile, in a medium-size skillet, melt 2 tablespoons of the butter over medium-high heat. Add the bread crumbs and pepper and saute for 3 to 4 minutes, until the crumbs are golden brown. Set the skillet aside.

Drain the pasta and transfer to a large serving bowl. Cut the remaining 2 tablespoons butter into bits. Add to the pasta along with the Romano, and season with salt, tossing until the butter melts. Sprinkle with the bread crumbs and serve. **SERVES 4**

penne ai tre formaggi

1 pound penne or penne rigate

4 ounces Gorgonzola dolce cheese, diced (*see Note*)

4 ounces mascarpone cheese

¼ cup heavy cream

Freshly ground pepper

¼ cup freshly grated Parmesan cheese

NOTE

This mild-flavored variety of blue-veined Gorgonzola can be purchased in cheese shops and specialty food stores.

A grown-up version of macaroni and cheese, this toothsome combination of Gorgonzola, mascarpone, and Parmesan will please even the most sophisticated palate.

Cook the pasta following the basic method (p. 52).

Meanwhile, in a large skillet, combine the Gorgonzola, mascarpone, and cream and cook over medium-low heat, stirring constantly, until the cheeses melt and the sauce is creamy. Season with pepper.

Drain the pasta and transfer to a large bowl. Add the sauce and toss until the pasta is well coated. Sprinkle with the Parmesan and serve. **SERVES 4 TO 6**

spaghetti with parmesan meatballs

In this full-flavored version of the classic, the meatballs are flavored with Parmesan cheese.

In a large skillet, heat 2 tablespoons of the oil over medium heat. Add the garlic and saute for 2 minutes. Using a slotted spoon, put the garlic on a plate. Set the pan with the garlic oil aside.

Prepare the Parmesan meatballs. In a large bowl, mix together all the ingredients, seasoning with salt and pepper. Shape into twenty-four 2-inch meatballs.

Add the remaining oil to the skillet. Over medium-high heat, cook the meatballs for 10 minutes, or until browned on all sides, transferring the meatballs to a plate as they brown.

Add the marinara sauce to the skillet. When it bubbles, return the meatballs to the skillet, reduce the heat and simmer, partially covered, for 5 minutes, or until heated through.

Cook the pasta following the basic method (p. 52). Drain, then transfer to a large serving dish. Spoon the meatballs and sauce over and top with the reserved garlic. Serve, passing the grated Parmesan on the side. **SERVES 6**

¼ cup olive oil

3 garlic cloves, sliced

PARMESAN MEATBALLS

1 pound each lean ground beef & pork

1 cup freshly grated Parmesan cheese

1 cup fresh bread crumbs

2 large eggs

½ cup beef broth

⅓ cup chopped onion

3 garlic cloves, minced

¼ cup each chopped fresh parsley & basil

Salt & ground pepper

1 recipe Slow-Cooked Marinara sauce (p. 18)

1 pound spaghetti

Freshly grated Parmesan cheese, for serving

savory beef & sausage ragu

This easy-to-prepare classic sauce has rich, long-cooked flavor even though it's ready in less than an hour.

Prepare the ragu: In a large nonreactive skillet, heat the oil over medium-high heat. Add the onion and carrot and cook, stirring, for 5 minutes, or until the onion is softened. Add the beef and sausage and cook, breaking up the meat with a wooden spoon, for about 6 minutes, or until the meat is no longer pink. Season with salt and pepper.

Add the tomatoes and bring to a simmer. Reduce the heat to medium-low and cook, stirring occasionally, for 35 minutes, or until thickened.

Meanwhile, cook the pasta following the basic method (p. 52). Drain well, then transfer to a large bowl.

Add the ragu and parsley to the pasta and toss well. Transfer to large shallow bowls and pass the Parmesan cheese on the side. **SERVES 4 TO 6**

RAGU

3 tablespoons olive oil

1 medium-size onion, finely chopped

1 carrot, chopped

½ pound lean ground beef

½ pound hot Italian sausage, casings removed & broken into chunks

Salt & freshly ground pepper

1 (28-ounce) can crushed tomatoes

1 pound pappardelle

¼ cup chopped fresh flat-leaf parsley or basil

Freshly grated Parmesan cheese, for serving

veal shank ragu with gremolata

- ¼ cup olive oil
- **6 meaty veal shanks (about 6 pounds), cut into 2-inch lengths**
- **Salt & freshly ground pepper**
- **1 medium-size onion, sliced**
- **1 medium-size carrot, chopped**
- **2 medium-size shallots, thinly sliced**
- **2 large garlic cloves, minced**
- **1½ to 2 cups chicken broth**
- **1 (28-ounce) can whole tomatoes, drained & chopped, juice reserved**

A generous amount of grated lemon zest makes an especially piquant gremolata that invigorates this meltingly rich osso buco-inspired sauce of braised veal shanks.

Prepare the ragu: In a large deep skillet or Dutch oven, heat the oil over medium-high heat. Working in batches, cook the veal until well browned on all sides, removing it to a plate as it browns. Season with salt and pepper and set aside.

Add the onion, carrot, and shallots to the pan and cook, stirring, for about 5 minutes, or until the onion and shallots are softened. Add the garlic and cook for 1 minute longer, or until fragrant. Pour 1 cup of the broth into the skillet and deglaze by bringing it to a boil and scraping to loosen any browned bits in the bottom of the pan. Return the veal to the pan and add the tomatoes with their juice and enough of the remaining broth to almost cover the meat.

Cover the pan and reduce the heat to low. Simmer gently for about 1½ hours, or until the meat is very tender when pierced with a fork.

Meanwhile, prepare the gremolata: In a small bowl, mix together the parsley, lemon zest, and garlic. Cover with plastic wrap and refrigerate.

Transfer the veal shanks to a large plate. When cool enough to handle, remove the meat from the bones and tear into chunky shreds. Scoop out the marrow from the bones and whisk into the sauce until blended. Return the shredded veal to the pan, stir in half the gremolata, and season to taste with salt and pepper if needed. Keep warm over low heat.

Meanwhile, cook the pasta following the basic method (p. 52). Drain well and transfer to a large platter or serving bowl. Spoon the ragu over the pasta, sprinkle with the remaining gremolata, and serve. **SERVES 6 TO 8**

GREMOLATA

**½ cup chopped fresh
flat-leaf parsley**

**Finely grated zest of
2 medium-size lemons**

2 garlic cloves, minced

**1 pound lasagne noodles,
broken into 1- to 2-inch
pieces**

beef daube with rigatoni

DAUBE

- ¼ cup olive oil
- 2 pounds stewing beef, cut into 1½-inch chunks
- Salt & freshly ground pepper
- 2 onions, coarsely chopped
- 1 small fennel bulb, trimmed & chopped, feathery tops reserved
- 4 large garlic cloves, minced
- 1 bottle dry red wine
- 5 fresh thyme sprigs or 1 teaspoon dried
- 2 bay leaves
- 1 strip orange zest
- ½ cup coarsely chopped pitted oil-cured olives

- 1 pound rigatoni

When preparing a stew with wine, use the same type of wine you plan to drink. Here, try a red Bandol from Provence or a Petit Syrah.

Prepare the daube: In a large deep skillet, heat the oil over medium-high heat. Brown the beef in batches, transferring it to a platter as it browns. Season with salt and pepper.

Add the onions and fennel to the pan and saute for 8 minutes, or until softened. Add the garlic and cook for 1 minute. Add 1 cup of the wine and bring to a boil, scraping to loosen any browned bits. Return the beef to the pan with the remaining wine, the thyme, bay leaves, and orange zest. Partially cover and simmer for 2½ hours, or until the meat is very tender when pierced with a fork. Season with salt and pepper. Add the olives and simmer for 30 minutes longer.

Cook the pasta following the basic method (p. 52). Drain, then transfer to a serving bowl. Top with the daube and garnish with the reserved fennel tops. **SERVES 8**

salmon with
tagliatelle & fried leeks

The salmon caviar garnish makes this elegant meal even more delectable and it ushers this dish into the realm of the extraordinary.

Prepare the fried leeks: Cut the leeks lengthwise in half. Wash under cold water and pat dry with paper towels. Cut the leeks lengthwise into fine julienne and spread out on a paper towel–lined baking sheet. Pat dry, then air-dry for 15 minutes.

In a large deep skillet or a deep-fryer, heat 2 to 3 inches of oil to 375°F.

In a large bowl, combine the flour, ½ teaspoon salt, and ¼ teaspoon pepper. Add the leeks, tossing until well coated with the flour. Working with a small handful of the leeks at a time, shake off the excess flour and carefully lower the leeks into the hot oil. Fry for 2 to 3 minutes, until golden brown. Remove the leeks with a slotted spoon and let drain on a paper towel–lined plate. Sprinkle with additional salt and pepper if desired and set aside.

Preheat a grill to high and brush with oil or preheat the broiler. Brush the salmon fillet with olive oil and season on both

FRIED LEEKS

3 large leeks, white part only

Vegetable oil, for deep-frying

2 tablespoons all-purpose flour

Salt & freshly ground pepper

1½-pounds skinless salmon fillet

Olive oil

Salt & freshly ground pepper

1 pound tagliatelle

1 cup heavy cream

2 tablespoons butter

Grated zest of 2 medium-size lemons

2 tablespoons fresh lemon juice

sides with salt and pepper. Grill the salmon for 4 to 6 minutes per side, until just cooked through. Break the salmon into bite-size chunks and put into a large bowl. Set aside and cover to keep warm.

Meanwhile, cook the pasta following the basic method (p. 52).

While the pasta is cooking, in a large deep skillet, bring the cream and butter to a boil over medium-high heat. Add the lemon zest and juice and cook, stirring, for about 2 minutes, or until the cream is reduced by half. Remove the pan from the heat.

Drain the pasta and transfer to the skillet. Add the chives and toss until the pasta is well coated with the sauce. Add the salmon and gently toss to mix.

To serve, divide the pasta among plates. Sprinkle the leeks on top, surround the leeks with some of the salmon caviar if using, and garnish with whole chives. **SERVES 6**

2 tablespoons snipped fresh chives, plus additional whole chives, for garnish

2 ounces salmon caviar, for garnish (optional)

fettuccine alle cozze

2 tablespoons olive oil

5 large garlic cloves, thinly sliced

Pinch of crushed red pepper flakes

4 pounds mussels, scrubbed well & debearded

1 cup dry white wine

1 pound spinach or plain fettuccine

¼ cup shredded fresh basil leaves

Salt & freshly ground pepper

If you make this dish in August, when tomatoes are at their peak, stir a cup or so of diced, ripe tomatoes into the sauce just before serving.

In a large nonreactive pot, heat the oil over medium-high heat. Add the garlic and red pepper flakes and saute for 1 minute. Add the mussels and wine to the pot. Cover and cook, using a slotted spoon to transfer the mussels to a large bowl as they open. Discard any that do not open.

Put about half of the mussels into a bowl, cover, and reserve for garnish. Remove the remaining mussels from their shells, working over the pot to catch their juices. Put the mussels into a large serving bowl; cover. Boil the mussel liquid for 3 to 4 minutes, until reduced by half.

Meanwhile, cook the pasta following the basic method (p. 52). Drain, then add to the mussels. Add the mussel liquid and basil, and season with salt and pepper, tossing until mixed. Top with the reserved mussels and serve. **SERVES 4 TO 6**

smoky chicken & vegetable pasta

4 small zucchini,
   halved lengthwise

1 small eggplant (about
   1 pound), cut into
   ½-inch-thick slices

1 red bell pepper,
   halved, cored & seeded

1 yellow bell pepper,
   halved, cored & seeded

1 medium-size red
   onion, cut into
   ½-inch-thick slices

½ cup extra-virgin
   olive oil

¼ cup lightly packed
   shredded fresh basil

2 tablespoons chopped
   fresh flat-leaf parsley

3 tablespoons fresh
   lemon juice

Salt & freshly ground
   pepper

To facilitate pitting the olives, place several olives on a work surface and press down on them with the flat side of a large knife until they split open. Then simply slip out the pits.

Preheat a gas grill to medium or prepare a medium-hot charcoal fire and brush with oil.

In a large bowl, combine the zucchini, eggplant, bell peppers, and onion. Add 3 tablespoons of the oil and toss until the vegetables are coated. Grill the vegetables, in batches if necessary, turning them, for 6 to 8 minutes, until tender and nicely marked.

Cut the zucchini into ½-inch-thick slices. Cut the bell peppers and eggplant into ½-inch-wide strips. Return all the grilled vegetables to the bowl and add the basil, parsley, ¼ cup of the oil, and the lemon juice. Season with salt and pepper and toss well. Let the vegetables marinate at room temperature while you prepare the chicken and pasta.

Brush the chicken on both sides with the remaining 1 tablespoon oil and season with salt and pepper. Grill, turning once, for 12 minutes, or until the chicken is just cooked through. Transfer to a plate and cover loosely with foil.

Cook the pasta following the basic method (p. 52).

Meanwhile, prepare the tapenade: In a food processor, combine the olives, anchovies, capers, garlic, thyme, oil, and lemon juice. Pulse until the mixture is very roughly chopped. Do not overprocess.

Drain the pasta, then add to the vegetables, tossing well. Divide the pasta mixture among serving plates. Cut each chicken breast crosswise into ½-inch-thick slices and arrange on top of the pasta. Top each serving with a small dollop of the tapenade.

SERVES 4

4 boneless skinless chicken breast halves (about 1¼ pounds)

½ pound fusilli

TAPENADE

1 cup Kalamata olives, pitted

4 anchovy fillets

3 tablespoons capers

1 garlic clove, minced

1 tablespoon fresh thyme leaves

¼ cup extra-virgin olive oil

1 tablespoon fresh lemon juice

pasta with roasted garlic & vinegar

- **3 medium-size heads garlic, tops sliced off**
- **¼ cup plus 2 tablespoons extra-virgin olive oil**
- **Salt & freshly ground pepper**
- **½ cup freshly grated Parmesan cheese**
- **3 scallions, thinly sliced**
- **1 tablespoon vinegar of choice, or more to taste**
- **1 pound pasta, any type**
- **2 tablespoons butter**
- **2 tablespoons chopped fresh parsley, for garnish**

The character of this dish alters depending on the vinegar used. Sherry vinegar lends a sprightly flavor, balsamic gives it a caramelized nuance, and tarragon vinegar adds an herbaceous undertone.

Preheat the oven to 375°F. Put the garlic into a small ovenproof dish, drizzle with 2 tablespoons of the oil, and season with salt and pepper. Cover tightly with foil and bake for 40 minutes, or until the garlic is soft. Set aside.

When cool enough to handle, squeeze out the garlic pulp from the cloves. Chop the softened garlic to form a rough puree and transfer to a small bowl. Stir in the Parmesan, scallions, vinegar, and the remaining ¼ cup oil.

Cook the pasta following the basic method (p. 52). Drain well and return to the pot. Add the butter, tossing until melted. Add the garlic mixture, season with salt and pepper, and toss, adding additional vinegar if desired. Transfer to a large serving bowl and sprinkle with the parsley. **SERVES 4 TO 6**

rotelle with minted walnut pesto

In this refreshing pesto variant, cream and butter replace most of the olive oil, while cool mint stands in for some of the basil.

Cook the pasta following the basic method (p. 52).

Meanwhile, prepare the minted walnut pesto: In a food processor, combine the mint, basil, parsley, walnuts, Parmesan, and garlic. Pulse until the ingredients are very finely chopped. With the machine running, add the cream and oil, pulsing just until blended.

Drain the pasta and return to the pot. Add the butter and toss until melted. Add the pesto, season with salt and pepper, and toss until the pasta is evenly coated with the pesto. Spoon the pasta into a large serving bowl and garnish with the mint sprigs. **SERVES 4 TO 6**

1 pound rotelle

MINTED WALNUT PESTO

1¼ cups lightly packed fresh mint leaves

¾ cup lightly packed fresh basil leaves

½ cup lightly packed fresh flat-leaf parsley

⅔ cup toasted walnuts

¼ cup freshly grated Parmesan cheese

3 large garlic cloves

⅓ cup heavy cream

3 tablespoons extra-virgin olive oil

3 tablespoons butter, cut into small pieces

Salt & freshly ground pepper

Mint sprigs, for garnish

pasta with tomatoes, fresh thyme & feta

- **1 pound pasta, any type**
- **2 pints cherry tomatoes, preferably a mix of red & yellow, halved**
- **1 cup crumbled feta cheese (4 ounces)**
- **3 tablespoons fresh thyme leaves or lemon thyme leaves**
- **3 large garlic cloves, minced**
- **¼ cup extra-virgin olive oil**
- **Salt & freshly ground pepper**

The piney flavor of fresh thyme and the salty feta cheese are a dramatic combination in this simple pasta salad.

Cook the pasta following the basic method.

In a large serving bowl, combine the cherry tomatoes, feta, thyme, garlic, and oil. Drain the pasta, then add to the tomato mixture. Season with salt and pepper and toss well. Serve immediately. **SERVES 6 TO 8**

BASIC PASTA COOKING METHOD

In a large pot, bring 4 quarts of cold water to a boil over high heat; add 2 tablespoons salt. Add the pasta and cook, stirring occasionally to prevent the pasta from sticking, until al dente. (Use the cooking time indicated on the pasta box as a guide.) When the pasta is al dente, it is considered firm to the bite—it should not be hard. Drain the pasta by pouring it into a colander; shake out the excess water. The pasta should not be rinsed unless specified in the recipe.

tagliatelle with wilted arugula & tomato

1 pound tagliatelle

¼ cup extra-virgin olive oil

½ cup brine-cured black olives, pitted & finely chopped

3 large garlic cloves, minced

⅛ teaspoon crushed red pepper flakes

Salt & freshly ground pepper

3 small bunches arugula, trimmed, washed & coarsely chopped

2 large tomatoes, peeled, seeded & cut into ½-inch dice, juice reserved

For a creamier, richer version of this fine, light pasta dish, stir in about one half cup of diced taleggio cheese along with the tomatoes.

Cook the pasta following the basic method (p. 52). Drain well.

In a large skillet, heat the oil over medium-high heat. Add the olives and garlic and saute for 2 minutes, or until the garlic is translucent. Stir in the red pepper flakes and season with salt and pepper. Add the arugula and saute for 2 minutes, or until wilted and softened.

Add the pasta and the tomatoes with their juice to the skillet. Toss over medium-high heat for 30 seconds, then transfer to a large shallow serving dish. **SERVES 4 TO 6**

penne with red & green peppers

There is nothing quite so tempting as silky roasted bell peppers glossed with fruity olive oil, slowly cooked down to a sauce, and tossed with hot pasta—simply luxurious.

In a very large skillet, heat the oil over medium-high heat. Add the roasted bell peppers and saute for 2 minutes. Stir in the garlic, sage, and red pepper flakes. Reduce the heat to low. Cover and cook, stirring occasionally, for 20 minutes, or until the bell peppers are very soft.

Meanwhile, cook the pasta following the basic method (p. 52). Drain well.

Add the pasta to the bell pepper sauce. Season with salt and pepper and toss well. Transfer to a shallow serving dish and garnish with the diced bell pepper. **SERVES 4 TO 6**

⅓ cup extra-virgin olive oil

3 large roasted red bell peppers, peeled, cored, seeded & cut into 1-inch-wide strips

3 large roasted green bell peppers, peeled, cored, seeded & cut into 1-inch-wide strips

1 large garlic clove, thinly sliced

1 tablespoon finely chopped fresh sage

Pinch of crushed red pepper flakes

1 pound penne

Salt & freshly ground pepper

¼ cup diced mixed red & green bell pepper, for garnish

rigatoni with garlicky broccoli sauce

Salt

1 pound rigatoni

1 large bunch broccoli, separated into 1-inch florets, stalks reserved for another use

½ cup extra-virgin olive oil

5 large garlic cloves, minced

3 anchovy fillets, chopped

1 tablespoon capers

½ teaspoon crushed red pepper flakes

Freshly ground pepper

2 tablespoons chopped fresh flat-leaf parsley

Cooking broccoli florets together with pasta is a traditional Southern Italian technique that eliminates the need to use a second pot.

In a large pot, bring 4 quarts of cold water to a boil over high heat. Add 2 tablespoons salt and the pasta. Cook for 4 minutes, then stir in the broccoli. Cook, stirring, for 5 minutes, until the pasta is al dente and the broccoli is tender. Drain, reserving ¼ cup of the pasta water. Return the pasta and broccoli to the pot and cover to keep warm.

In a small skillet, heat the oil over medium-high heat. Add the garlic and anchovies and cook, stirring, for 2 minutes, or until the garlic is golden. Add the capers; cook 1 minute. Add the red pepper flakes and season with salt and pepper.

Pour the garlic mixture over the pasta and toss, adding pasta water, 1 tablespoon at a time, if the pasta seems dry. Season with salt and pepper. Spoon into a large serving bowl and sprinkle with the parsley. **SERVES 4 TO 6**

ziti with artichokes & toasted almonds

Ricotta cheese makes a full-bodied, creamy sauce for this dish of tender, fragrant stewed artichokes and golden toasted almonds.

In a large skillet, heat the oil over medium-high heat. Add the garlic and saute for 1 minute, or until golden. Stir in the artichokes and wine and cook, partially covered, for 20 minutes, or until the artichokes are tender. Stir in the basil and parsley, and season with salt and pepper.

Meanwhile, cook the pasta following the basic method (p. 52). Drain well, reserving ¼ cup of the pasta water.

In a large serving bowl, mix together the ricotta and 2 tablespoons of the reserved pasta water. Add the pasta and the artichoke mixture and toss until well coated with the ricotta. If the mixture seems dry, stir in additional pasta water, 1 tablespoon at a time. Sprinkle with the almonds and serve.

SERVES 4 TO 6

¼ cup extra-virgin olive oil

3 large garlic cloves, minced

2 (10-ounce) packages frozen artichoke hearts, thawed

1 cup white wine, such as a dry riesling

2 tablespoons chopped fresh basil

2 tablespoons chopped fresh flat-leaf parsley

Salt & freshly ground pepper

1 pound ziti or gemelli

1¼ cups ricotta cheese

½ cup slivered almonds, toasted

gemelli with asparagus & roasted mushrooms

Portobello mushrooms lend this dish a deep, woodsy flavor, while tender asparagus contributes a fresh springlike flavor.

Preheat the oven to 425°F. In a 13-x-9-inch baking dish, toss the mushrooms with 2 tablespoons of the oil, and season with salt and pepper. Roast the mushrooms, stirring once, for about 15 minutes, or until browned and tender. Set aside and cover to keep warm.

Meanwhile, in a large pot, bring 4 quarts of cold water to a boil over high heat. Add the asparagus and blanch for 1 minute. Using a slotted spoon, remove to a large serving bowl and cover.

Add 2 tablespoons salt and the pasta to the boiling water. Cook the pasta following the basic method (p. 52). Drain well and add to the asparagus.

Add the mushrooms, the remaining 3 tablespoons oil, the Romano, and lemon juice to the pasta. Season with salt and pepper and toss until mixed. Serve with the additional cheese on the side. **SERVES 6 TO 8**

¾ pound small portobello mushrooms, stems removed, cleaned, halved & cut into ¼-inch-thick slices

¼ cup plus 1 tablespoon extra-virgin olive oil

Salt & freshly ground pepper

1½ pounds pencil asparagus, tough ends removed & cut into 1½-inch lengths

1 pound gemelli or ziti

⅓ cup freshly grated Pecorino Romano cheese, plus additional for serving

1 tablespoon fresh lemon juice

fusilli with tomato-eggplant sauce

TOMATO-EGGPLANT SAUCE

- 1½ pounds small Italian eggplants, peeled & cut into ¼-inch-thick slices
- 2 large garlic cloves, minced
- Salt & freshly ground pepper
- ¼ cup plus 2 tablespoons olive oil
- 1 medium-size red onion, finely chopped
- 1 (28-ounce) can crushed tomatoes
- 2 tablespoons chopped fresh marjoram

- 1 pound fusilli
- 1 cup grated ricotta salata or feta cheese (4 ounces), for serving

It's worth the effort to seek out small Italian eggplants for this Sicilian dish. Their lack of seeds and sweet flavor make all the difference.

Prepare the tomato-eggplant sauce: In a large bowl, put the eggplant and garlic. Season with salt and pepper, add ¼ cup of the oil, and toss. Let marinate for 10 minutes.

Preheat the broiler. Arrange the eggplant slices in a single layer on the broiler pan, leaving any oil and the garlic in the bowl. Broil, turning once, for 10 minutes, or until tender. Return the eggplant to the bowl with the garlic and set aside.

In a large skillet, heat the remaining 2 tablespoons oil over medium-high heat. Add the onion and saute for 5 minutes, or until softened. Add the tomatoes and simmer for 25 minutes, or until the sauce has reduced slightly. Stir in the marjoram.

Cook the pasta following the basic method (p. 52). Drain. Stir the pasta into the tomato sauce. Add the eggplant, season with salt and pepper, and toss. Transfer to a deep bowl and serve, passing the ricotta salata separately. **SERVES 4 TO 6**

capellini pancakes

These fluffy pancakes can be topped either with poached fruit or sauteed wild mushrooms. And they are equally luscious simply drizzled with melted butter and sprinkled with sugar.

Cook the pasta following the basic method (p. 52). Drain and set aside.

Melt 2 tablespoons of the butter. In a small bowl, whisk together the flour and baking soda. In a large bowl, whisk together the sour cream, eggs, and melted butter. Add the flour mixture and stir just until combined. Stir in the capellini.

In a large nonstick skillet, melt the remaining 1 tablespoon butter over medium heat. Drop the batter by ¼ cupfuls. Cook the pancakes for 3 to 4 minutes, until the underside is golden and tiny bubbles appear on the surface. Flip the pancakes and cook for 1 minute longer, or until golden on the second side. Transfer to a heated platter and cover loosely with foil. Continue making pancakes with the remaining batter, using additional butter if needed. Serve hot. **SERVES 4**

½ pound capellini, broken into 2-inch lengths

3 tablespoons butter, plus additional if needed

1 cup all-purpose flour

1 teaspoon baking soda

2 cups sour cream

4 large eggs

elbow macaroni frittata

1 pound elbow macaroni

2 ounces thinly sliced pancetta

8 large eggs

½ cup freshly grated Pecorino Romano cheese

3 large garlic cloves, minced

2 tablespoons chopped fresh flat-leaf parsley

Salt & freshly ground pepper

2 tablespoons butter

1 roasted red bell pepper, peeled, cored, seeded & cut into 1-inch-wide strips (optional)

Serve this soothing pasta for a tempting dinner, brunch, or even as an unusual hors d'oeuvre.

Preheat the oven to 450°F. Cook the pasta following the basic method (p. 52). Drain well and set aside.

Cook the pancetta in a large skillet over medium heat until crisp and browned. Drain on a paper towel–lined plate, then cut into ½-inch pieces.

In a large bowl, whisk together the eggs, Romano, garlic, parsley, and pancetta, and season with salt and pepper. Add the pasta and mix well. In a 10-inch ovenproof skillet, melt the butter over medium heat. Pour in the egg mixture, spreading it evenly, and cook for about 5 minutes, or until the bottom is golden and the center is almost set. Transfer the skillet to the oven and bake for 2 to 4 minutes, until the eggs are set.

Run a rubber spatula around the edges of the pan to loosen the frittata, then invert it onto a serving plate. Arrange the bell pepper strips on top if using, and cut the frittata into wedges. Serve hot, warm, or at room temperature. **SERVES 4 TO 6**

maccheroni al forno alla rustica

TOMATO SAUCE

2 tablespoons butter

1 large onion, thinly sliced

1 (14-ounce) can diced tomatoes, undrained

1 tablespoon chopped fresh thyme

Salt & freshly ground pepper

1 large eggplant (1½ to 2 pounds), peeled, cut into ½-inch-thick slices & into 1-inch-wide strips

¼ cup plus 1 tablespoon extra-virgin olive oil

Salt & freshly ground pepper

1 pound elbow macaroni

¼ cup freshly grated Parmesan cheese

4 ounces smoked fresh mozzarella cheese, very thinly sliced

Melted smoked mozzarella and crispy roasted eggplant give this meatless entrée a rich, earthy flavor that is at once inviting and comforting.

Preheat the oven to 450°F.

Prepare the tomato sauce: In a large skillet, melt the butter over medium heat. Add the onion and saute for 5 minutes, or until softened. Add the tomatoes and thyme and season with salt and pepper. Cook for 20 minutes, or until the tomatoes have cooked down into a sauce. Set aside.

Meanwhile, in a large bowl, toss the eggplant with ¼ cup of the oil. Divide the eggplant between two jelly-roll pans or baking sheets, spreading the strips in a single layer. Season with salt and pepper. Roast the eggplant, turning once, for 15 minutes, or until golden. Transfer to a rack to cool. Reduce the oven temperature to 400°F.

Cook the pasta following the basic method (p. 52). Drain well, then return to the pot. Add the Parmesan, tomato sauce, and eggplant to the pasta and toss until combined.

Brush the bottom of a shallow 2-quart baking dish with the remaining 1 tablespoon oil. Spoon in about half of the pasta mixture, spreading it into an even layer. Cover with half the mozzarella and the remaining pasta. Top with the remaining mozzarella.

Bake the pasta for about 20 minutes, or until light golden brown on top. Let stand for about 10 minutes before serving.

SERVES 4 TO 6

baked ziti with veal & mozzarella

RAGU

¼ cup olive oil

1 small red onion, finely chopped

1 large garlic clove, minced

½ pound ground veal

Salt & freshly ground pepper

1 (28-ounce) can crushed tomatoes

1 tablespoon chopped fresh marjoram or 1 teaspoon dried

1 pound ziti

8 ounces unsalted fresh mozzarella cheese, grated (about 2 cups)

Fresh mozzarella cheese is a delectably creamy foil for this full-flavored ragu.

Prepare the ragu: In a large nonreactive skillet, heat the oil over medium-high heat. Add the onion and saute for 3 minutes, or until softened. Add the garlic and saute for 1 minute longer. Add the veal and cook, breaking up the meat with a wooden spoon, for about 5 minutes, or until it is no longer pink. Season with salt and pepper.

Add the tomatoes and marjoram and bring to a simmer. Reduce the heat to medium-low and let the sauce cook, stirring occasionally, for about 30 minutes, or until it has thickened.

Preheat the oven to 375°F.

Meanwhile, cook the pasta following the basic method (p. 52). Drain and transfer to a large bowl. Add the sauce and toss. Transfer to an ungreased 2-quart baking dish and sprinkle with the mozzarella. Bake for about 15 minutes, or until the cheese melts and the top is light golden brown. Let rest for 5 minutes before serving. **SERVES 4 TO 6**

lasagne with goat cheese & chard

Salt

1 pound fresh lasagne noodles

2 tablespoons butter

2 tablespoons extra-virgin olive oil

4 large garlic cloves, minced

1 teaspoon fresh thyme leaves

2 large bunches Swiss chard (about 2 pounds), trimmed, washed & coarsely chopped

1 recipe Quick Tomato-Basil Sauce (p. 17)

Freshly ground pepper

¾ pound fresh goat cheese, crumbled (about 3 cups)

¾ cup freshly grated Parmesan cheese

Simplicity and freshness are the key to a truly magnificent lasagne.

Preheat the oven to 400°F. Fill a large basin with ice water and cover the work surface with a clean kitchen towel.

In a large pot, bring 4 quarts of cold water to a boil over high heat. Add 2 tablespoons salt and half the noodles. Cook, stirring, until the water returns to a boil. Transfer the noodles to the ice water to stop the cooking. Place the noodles on the towel in a single layer. Cook the remaining noodles.

In a large skillet, melt the butter with the oil over medium-high heat. Add the garlic and thyme and saute for 1 minute. Add the chard and saute for 7 minutes, or until wilted. Stir in the tomato sauce and season with salt and pepper.

Cover the bottom of a 13-x-9-inch baking dish with one third of the noodles. Spread one third of the chard mixture over and top with half the goat cheese. Continue layering, ending with the chard mixture. Sprinkle with the Parmesan.

Bake for 25 minutes, or until bubbling. **SERVES 6 TO 8**

pasta with white beans & broccoli rabe

Broccoli rabe is also known as broccoli rape, broccoli raab, and rapini. It is a member of the broccoli family and has a slightly bitter flavor.

Preheat the oven to 425°F. In a large pot, bring 4 quarts of cold water to a boil over high heat. Add 2 tablespoons salt and the pasta. Cook, stirring, for 9 minutes. Stir in the broccoli rabe and cook for 1 minute, or until the pasta is al dente. Drain, reserving ⅓ cup of the pasta water. Return the pasta and broccoli rabe to the pot and cover to keep warm.

Meanwhile, cook the pancetta in a large skillet over medium heat until crisp and browned. Drain on a paper towel–lined plate, then cut into ½-inch pieces.

Add the pancetta to the pasta along with the reserved pasta water, the beans, tomatoes, Parmesan, and garlic, and season with salt and pepper, mixing well. Spoon the mixture into a shallow 3-quart baking dish and drizzle with the oil. Bake for 25 minutes, or until the edges are golden brown. **SERVES 4 TO 6**

Salt

1 pound penne

1 large bunch broccoli rabe, trimmed & cut into 1-inch pieces

¼ pound thinly sliced pancetta

2 (15-ounce) cans cannellini beans, drained & rinsed

3 large tomatoes, peeled, seeded & cut into ½-inch dice, juice reserved

¾ cup freshly grated Parmesan cheese

4 large garlic cloves, minced

Freshly ground pepper

1 tablespoon extra-virgin olive oil

roasted vegetable & macaroni timballo

1 medium-size eggplant (1 to 1½ pounds), cut into ½-inch-thick slices & then into 1-inch-wide strips

2 medium-size zucchini, cut into ¼-inch-thick slices

10 ounces button mushrooms, trimmed, cleaned & quartered

1 large red bell pepper, halved, cored, seeded & cut into thin strips

3 tablespoons olive oil

Salt & freshly ground pepper

1 pound elbow macaroni

2 cups Savory Meat and Sausage Ragu (p. 39) or Slow-Cooked Marinara Sauce (p. 18)

8 ounces mozzarella cheese, grated (2 cups)

In this festive timballo-shaped pasta dish, puff pastry encloses a robust mixture of pasta, tomato-meat sauce, roasted vegetables, and mozzarella cheese.

Preheat the oven to 450°F.

In a large roasting pan, toss together the eggplant, zucchini, mushrooms, bell pepper, and oil, and season with salt and pepper. Spread the vegetables out in single layer and roast, tossing once, for about 15 minutes, or until browned and tender. Transfer the pan to a wire rack to cool. Reduce the oven temperature to 375°F.

Cook the pasta following the basic method (p. 52). Drain well, then transfer to a very large bowl. Add the roasted vegetables, the ragu, mozzarella, Parmesan, and eggs, stirring until well combined. Set aside.

Using the bottom of a 10-inch springform pan as a guide, cut out two 10-inch rounds from two of the puff pastry sheets, reserving the scraps. Cut the remaining pastry sheet lengthwise

½ cup freshly grated
  Parmesan cheese

2 large eggs, well beaten

3 frozen puff pastry
  sheets (one and a half
  17½-ounce packages),
  thawed according to
  package directions

in half. Line the springform pan with one of the pastry rounds. Line the sides of the springform pan with the pastry strips (they will not reach all the way around), allowing the pastry to extend over the top of the pan. Cut and fit some of the pastry to fill in any gaps. Pinch all the dough edges together to seal the seams, then trim the top pastry edge slightly beyond the rim of the pan. Spoon the pasta mixture into the crust, compressing it gently. (Put any extra filling in a small baking dish and bake alongside the timballo.) Top with the remaining pastry round. Pinch the edges of the dough to seal. Cut or twist some of the pastry scraps into decorative shapes and arrange on top of the timballo, attaching them with a little cold water. With a small knife, cut one or two steam vents in the top.

Bake the timballo for 50 to 55 minutes, until the crust is golden brown. If the top crust begins to brown too quickly, cover loosely with foil. Let the timballo rest, uncovered, for 10 minutes. To serve, gently remove the sides of the pan and transfer to a platter. Cut into wedges and serve. **SERVES 6 TO 8**

orzo pudding with pistachios & raisins

This luscious pudding will satiate comfort food enthusiasts with its creamy texture, and sophisticates with its mix of golden raisins, pistachio nuts, and orange flower water.

In a large nonstick saucepan, bring the milk to a boil over medium-high heat. Immediately stir in the orzo, sugar, cinnamon stick, and salt. When the milk returns to a simmer, reduce the heat to medium-low. Cover and cook, stirring, for 20 minutes, or until the orzo is very tender.

Meanwhile, in a small bowl, whisk together the cream and egg yolks until smooth.

Gradually add the egg yolk mixture to the orzo, whisking constantly. Stir in the raisins, orange flower water, and orange zest. Cook, uncovered, for 3 minutes longer.

Remove the cinnamon stick, then divide the pudding among small bowls or parfait glasses. Garnish with the pistachios and serve warm, at room temperature, or cold. **SERVES 6 TO 8**

6 cups milk

1 pound orzo

⅔ cup sugar

One 2-inch piece cinnamon stick

Pinch of salt

½ cup heavy cream

2 large egg yolks

½ cup golden raisins

1 tablespoon orange flower water *(see Note)*

½ teaspoon finely grated orange zest

⅓ cup finely chopped pistachio nuts, for garnish

NOTE

Orange flower water is available in specialty food stores.

baked vermicelli with ricotta & grapes

The flavors here, reminiscent of a ricotta cheese-cake, are both comforting and luxurious, with the added surprise of plump, juicy red grapes.

Preheat the oven to 325°F. Butter 6 to 8 ramekins or a shallow 1½-quart baking dish.

In a large skillet, melt the butter over medium-high heat. Add the vermicelli and cook, stirring, for 5 minutes, or until the pasta is golden. Add the water, bring to a simmer, and cook for about 7 minutes, or until the water is absorbed. Add the cream and the ½ cup sugar. Simmer, stirring, for 5 minutes, or until the cream is reduced by about a third.

Meanwhile, in a large bowl, whisk the eggs until frothy. Stir in the ricotta and ½ teaspoon of the cinnamon.

Add the vermicelli mixture to the ricotta and mix. Spoon into the prepared baking dishes and place the grapes on top. Sprinkle with sugar and the remaining ¼ teaspoon cinnamon.

Bake for 45 minutes, or until golden brown. Serve warm or at room temperature. **SERVES 6 TO 8**

- ¼ cup (½ stick) **unsalted butter**
- ½ pound **egg vermicelli, broken into 2-inch lengths**
- 2 cups **cold water**
- 2 cups **heavy cream**
- ½ cup **sugar plus additional sugar for sprinkling**
- 4 large **eggs**
- 1 pound **ricotta cheese**
- ¾ teaspoon **ground cinnamon**
- 3 cups **seedless red grapes**

couscous
crème brûlée

2 cups half-and-half

2 cups heavy cream

½ vanilla bean, split
  lengthwise

¾ cup milk

½ cup couscous

1 tablespoon honey

Pinch of salt

8 large egg yolks

½ cup granulated sugar

¾ cup packed light
  brown sugar

In this elegant dessert, a glasslike caramel topping conceals a silky smooth custard and an unexpected layer of honey-flavored couscous.

Preheat the oven to 300°F. Place one rack in the center of the oven.

In a medium-size saucepan, combine the half-and-half, cream, and vanilla bean and bring to a simmer over medium heat. Remove from the heat, cover the pan, and set aside.

In a small saucepan, bring the milk to a simmer over medium heat. Stir in the couscous, honey, and salt. Cover the pan and remove from the heat. Let stand for about 10 minutes, or until the couscous has absorbed all the milk. Fluff the couscous with a fork and set aside.

In a medium-size bowl, whisk together the egg yolks and granulated sugar. Remove the vanilla bean from the cream mixture and using the tip of a knife, scrape out the vanilla seeds and whisk them into the cream. If the cream is no longer hot to the touch, reheat briefly. Slowly whisk the cream mixture into

into the egg yolks, then pour the custard through a strainer set over a clean medium-size bowl.

Place eight ¾-cup ramekins or custard cups in a large roasting pan. Divide the couscous among the ramekins and top with the custard, dividing it evenly. Pour enough hot water into the roasting pan to come halfway up the sides of the ramekins. Bake the custards for 30 to 40 minutes, or until just set. (A paring knife inserted into the center will come out clean.) Transfer the custards to a wire rack to cool completely.

Cover the custards with plastic wrap and refrigerate for at least 3 hours, or overnight.

To serve, preheat the broiler. Press the brown sugar through a small strainer, then spoon in an even layer over the custards. Place the ramekins on a broiler pan and broil 3 inches from the heat, for about 30 seconds, or until the sugar melts. Watch carefully to prevent the sugar from burning. Serve immediately.

SERVES 8

types of pasta

		pesto & light sauces	tomato sauces	cream sauces	ragus	seafood sauces	salads & vegetables
strands	BUCATINI	*	*			*	
	CAPELLINI	*	*				
	LONG FUSILLI	*	*			*	
	SPAGHETTI	*	*			*	
	VERMICELLI	*	*				
ribbons	FETTUCCINE	*	*	*		*	*
	LASAGNE		*	*	*		
	LINGUINE	*	*	*		*	
	PAPPARDELLE		*	*	*		*
	TAGLIATELLE	*	*	*		*	*
tubes	DITALINI	*		*			
	ELBOWS	*	*	*		*	*
	PENNE	*	*	*	*	*	*
	RIGATONI		*	*	*	*	
	TUBETTI	*		*			
	ZITI	*	*	*	*	*	*
shapes	CONCHIGLIE	*	*		*	*	*
	FARFALLE	*	*	*	*		*
	FUSILLI	*	*	*	*		*
	GEMELLI		*		*	*	*
	ORECCHIETTE		*		*	*	*
	ROTELLE	*	*		*		*

weights

Ounces and Pounds	Metric Equivalents
$\frac{1}{4}$ ounce	7 grams
$\frac{1}{3}$ ounce	10 g
$\frac{1}{2}$ ounce	14 g
1 ounce	28 g
$1\frac{1}{2}$ ounces	42 g
$1\frac{3}{4}$ ounces	50 g
2 ounces	57 g
3 ounces	85 g
$3\frac{1}{2}$ ounces	100 g
4 ounces ($\frac{1}{4}$ pound)	114 g
6 ounces	170 g
8 ounces ($\frac{1}{2}$ pound)	227 g
9 ounces	250 g
16 ounces (1 pound)	464 g

temperatures

°F (Fahrenheit)	°C (Centigrade or Celsius)
32 (water freezes)	0
200	95
212 (water boils)	100
250	120
275	135
300 (slow oven)	150
325	160
350 (moderate oven)	175
375	190
400 (hot oven)	205
425	220
450 (very hot oven)	232
475	245
500 (extremely hot oven)	260

liquid measures

Spoons and Cups	Metric Equivalents
$\frac{1}{4}$ tsp.	1.23 milliliters
$\frac{1}{2}$ tsp.	2.5 ml
$\frac{3}{4}$ tsp.	3.7 ml
1 tsp.	5 ml
1 Tbs. (3 tsp.)	15 ml
2 Tbs. (1 ounce)	30 ml
$\frac{1}{4}$ cup	60 ml
$\frac{1}{3}$ cup	80 ml
$\frac{1}{2}$ cup	120 ml
$\frac{2}{3}$ cup	160 ml
$\frac{3}{4}$ cup	180 ml
1 cup	235 ml
2 cups	475 ml
3 cups	710 ml
4 cups (1 quart)	1 liter
4 quarts (1 gallon)	3.75 liters

(tsp.: teaspoon/Tbs.: tablespoon)

length

U.S. Measurements	Metric Equivalents
$\frac{1}{8}$ inch	3 mm
$\frac{1}{4}$ inch	6 mm
$\frac{3}{8}$ inch	1 cm
$\frac{1}{2}$ inch	1.2 cm
$\frac{3}{4}$ inch	2 cm
1 inch	2.5 cm
$1\frac{1}{4}$ inches	3.1 cm
$1\frac{1}{2}$ inches	3.7 cm
2 inches	5 cm
3 inches	7.5 cm
4 inches	10 cm
5 inches	12.5 cm

approximate equivalents

1 kilogram is slightly more than 2 pounds
1 liter is slightly more than 1 quart
1 meter is slightly over 3 feet
1 centimeter is approximately $\frac{3}{8}$ inch

index